Published by Meadowcroft Publishing

Cover design by info@amapopico.com and Book Cover Zone.

MAP OF CHALK GAP VILLAGE

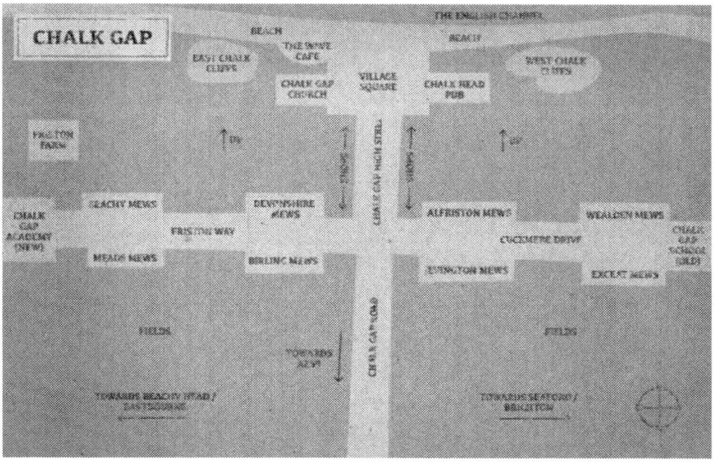

CHALK GAP BODY IDENTIFIED

A man's body found at the bottom of West Chalk Cliff has been identified as local supply teacher **Jackson King**, 34.

Emergency services recovered the body from the cliff in Chalk Gap village, near Eastbourne, at about 7am on Friday, 29th January.

Sussex Police and Eastbourne coastguard teams were involved in the incident.

A police spokeswoman said: "Emergency services were called to West Chalk Cliff after reports of a body of a man had been found."

Jackson is survived by his wife, Mary King, and baby son, Joshua. The funeral will take place on Friday 12th February at Chalk Gap Church. Family flowers only. Donations in memory of Jackson can be made to the Mental Health Foundation.

1

The two cliffs surrounding Chalk Gap village are beautiful, but there's a certain sadness that comes with the thought that lives have come to a tragic end up there. The death rates are much lower than Birling Gap to our West, and certainly Beachy Head to our East (the third most common suicide spot in the world), but they still happen occasionally.

Chalk Gap had recently been rocked by the death of a local man, Jackson King, who'd been found at the bottom of West Chalk Cliff a couple of weeks ago: the first death at our cliffs for about three years.

This didn't even occur to me that Thursday late afternoon in mid February, as my student library assistant, Noah, and I trekked the heights of the cliff, me struggling to breathe and him bounding giddily ahead in his excitable teenage manner. We'd finished school for the February break and I'd been convinced to celebrate by participating in a hike up to the West Chalk summit.

I shouldn't really call him my student librarian. He still is, of course, while he remains at our school as a post-16 student, and this is something he's extremely proud of. But even more proudly, he now calls himself my foster brother, after Mum and Dad started fostering him last year. I let Mum and Dad think I'm not happy with this label, but really I don't mind it. Even when Mum uses it against me in situations like this.

'You'll have to take your foster brother up the cliffs if he wants to go, me and your Dad can't be doing that at our age!' was my greeting earlier today when I arrived at the Chalk Head, our family's pub. 'I know he's 17, but I'd feel happier if you went with him, Edward.' I didn't get much choice in the matter, and off we went.

'Edward, do you think we're near where Mr King jumped from then?' I'd only just got Noah out of the habit of calling me 'Edward' rather than 'Sir,' as he'd always called me at school. And similarly, Jackson King's brief time as a supply teacher at our school had earned him his full name, even after death.

Jackson, a Maths cover teacher, worked with us for a few weeks last year, before going to work at another school in Eastbourne until his recent tragic death. But Noah knew him and had taken a keen interest in the case since it happened. Of course.

'Noah, this is why you wanted to come up here, isn't it?'

'Oh yes, of course,' he replied cheerfully, with no element of guilt or shame. 'I find it really interesting. Do you know he just walked out of his lesson in the middle of the school day?'

I did know. Everyone knew. Barely anything of note ever happens in our little village, yet six months after our village Head Teacher's murder, and mere weeks after what the press (and Noah) had named 'The Snow Day Murders,' Chalk Gap was in the headlines again following Jackson's death.

The local media used it as evidence of the pressure teachers are under, and this theory had started to gain traction, putting our village in a wider spotlight via Jackson. The Eastbourne school involved fought back by saying that their supply teachers aren't under any pressure, with no planning or marking expected, instead stating it was a more personal tragedy.

There was even a rumour that a note was left at school reception for Jackson that day and hand delivered to him, suggesting that the content of the note must have led to Jackson's actions. But no note was ever mentioned in the inquest, and this part of the story had been forgotten by most, with the death being ruled as a suicide.

I had previously heard that Jackson had a history of 'mental health problems,' through the rumours which passed round our village, with that ominous label being assigned to him in the muttered, whispered, conspiratorial way people do when they aren't comfortable discussing mental health. Some, discussing it more openly, thought the pressure of being a father, along with a stressful job and a history of mental health problems, had pushed the already ill man to the brink.

Either way, the suicide caused much local gossip. The Kings have lived in Chalk Gap for years, even though Jackson's mum is the only one still living here now. She owns the village shop – where apparently takings have gone through the roof the past couple of weeks. At least it wasn't a murder this time. But that didn't stop Noah.

'Since I started my Psychology course I'm really interested in mental health,' he continued. 'I've been reading all about it – I want to look into why he jumped.'

I didn't quite know what to say to that. Here was Noah trying to investigate once again, just like he did in the last case. At least he didn't seem to think he was in the pages of a murder mystery novel this time.

'Edward, I think the spot Mr King jumped from is just over there.'

I was so preoccupied in my thoughts that I barely noticed that he'd started to walk towards the cliff tops on our left. 'What makes you say that?' I asked as I finally looked in the direction he was going.

'Because that's Mr King's wife stood right on the cliff edge, I've seen her picture online,' he called back over his shoulder. 'Do you think she's going to jump too?'

2

'Noah, wait!' I shouted desperately as I chased after him. I knew what Noah was like, and if this lady was genuinely in distress he might not be the best person to approach her. A slight wind had picked up, and I felt it in my face as I pursued him.

He didn't stop as he moved towards her. She had her back to us and stood perfectly still, looking straight ahead into nothingness. She was still a good distance away - how had he even recognised her? I'd have to worry about that later – I couldn't let him reach her.

'Noah!' I shouted in the firmest voice I could muster, whilst trying not to be so loud that the cliff edge lady would hear me.

To my surprise, it worked. He stopped dead in his tracks and turned to face me. 'Yes, what's the matter?'

Ignoring the stitch I could now feel in my side, I waited until I reached him before speaking. 'You can't just go and take someone by surprise, Noah, you might make them jump.'

Bad choice of words, especially to literal Noah.

'No, that's what I was trying to prevent.'

'I mean, we can't startle her,' I clarified. 'I know you want to help, but we don't know why she's on the cliff edge.'

Didn't we? A grieving young widow, with a late husband who had suddenly and inexplicably taken his own life. I knew barely anything about Mary King outside of a few comments from Mum, but it wasn't beyond the realms of possibility that she was considering following her husband in death. Or she could just be visiting the spot where it happened, to pay her respects. Although she did seem very close to the edge.

'Let's just say hello and check she's okay then,' Noah said, making maybe his most sensible suggestion so far.

'Alright then,' I agreed. 'But I'll do it.' Even a normal hello from well meaning but overly loud Noah could still alarm her.

I took a deep breath as I reached close enough for her to hear me, after persuading Noah to stay back a little. I looked ahead at the beautiful blue nothingness of the sky and sea in front of us, and hoped that this would go well.

'Good evening,' I called out, immediately conscious of my own voice in the air. 'It's lovely up here, isn't it?'

Why on earth did I say that? Of course it isn't lovely if you're marking the spot where your husband died.

The lady turned round to look at me. The first thing I noticed was that she was wearing sunglasses. But somehow, I could still see the calm in her face - she didn't look distressed or upset, or in any danger to herself. Had I got this wrong?

'It is lovely, yes,' she replied. Her voice was quiet and serene – I could only just hear it above the wind in the air. She suddenly seemed to notice my concern, and smiled at me as if to reassure me that she was okay. 'I'm probably a little close to the edge here, aren't I?'

'A little,' I said as she started to walk towards me. The sunglasses obscured my impression, but she looked pretty as her smile lit up her face, and wore a bright summer dress that was either a few months too early or a few months too late to wear, but still looked stylish. I knew that Jackson King was a couple of years older than me, but she looked younger. Was this even Jackson's wife, or had Noah got it wrong?

'I'm sorry to worry you. It's just…' she stopped herself suddenly. 'My husband died here a few weeks ago.'

Noah *was* right. I'm trying to get better at managing a range of social situations, and I've certainly had more experience of this lately. But this was still out of my comfort zone.

'Yes, I knew him a little, I'm sorry for your loss,' I managed to say, hoping it was the right thing.

Whilst hoping even more that Noah, stood back watching us and certain *not* to say the right thing, wouldn't come and join us.

She looked at me for a moment through her sunglasses. 'Of course, I've just realised who you are... you solved the murder of the Head Teacher and the snow day ones, didn't you?'

'Yes he did!' I heard a voice behind me and turned my head to see Noah bounding over. 'He solved the murders brilliantly. The first one was my -'

'I'm Edward, and this is Noah,' I said, cutting him off as quickly as I possibly could.

'I'm Mary. In fact, isn't it your family who run the village pub? We have the wake there tomorrow after the funeral.'

That was right. Mum had told me all about it whilst gossiping about Jackson, Dad was picking songs that were suitable for a funeral (he was insisting on *Spirit in the Sky*), while my brother was doing all the preparations by himself.

'Then of course, I already know all about Noah,' she continued as she smiled. 'Jackson really enjoyed teaching you Maths briefly – you're quite the character, I heard.'

'Yes!' Noah punched the air as he beamed with pride. 'Teachers always like me the best. I liked Mr. King. He wasn't my absolute favourite teacher, but I'm sorry that he's dead.'

Mary must have seen the look of horror on my

face but she didn't miss a beat. 'Thank you, Noah. And don't worry, Jackson was used to that. He was never anyone's favourite when he was only in each school for a few weeks at a time.'

'He was a very good teacher though,' Noah replied. 'Just that everyone in the class was really horrible and wouldn't let him teach.'

Mary laughed. 'Again, he was used to that. The perils of being a cover teacher.'

'Everyone should be nice to their teachers, I am,' Noah asserted before he paused, seeming to be deep in thought. I felt a sudden sense of dread as to what he might say next.

'Do you think he killed himself because he hated his job?' There it was.

There was a pause for a moment, no one spoke. Even Noah was silent – I'd like to think he'd realised that he'd spoke insensitively.

Mary slowly removed her sunglasses and for the first time, I could feel the pain in her red, swollen eyes.

'Noah, I'm afraid you're mistaken,' she spoke slowly and her voice was quiet again, but no serenity this time. 'My husband didn't kill himself. He was murdered.'

3

'Murdered?' I could tell that Noah could barely contain his excitement as Mary King's words rang in the air.

'Murdered,' Mary repeated, her voice firm.

'But that can't be right,' Noah continued. 'I've been reading all about it – it was ruled suicide. They've made their final decision now – it's the funeral tomorrow.' Noah spoke as if he was passing information on to someone who didn't know, not in conversation with the widow of the funeral's subject.

'I know, but they're wrong,' Mary said. She fiddled with the sunglasses in her hands. 'I really want to speak to you more about this, but I can't now.' She placed the sunglasses back on her face and started to walk past us away from the cliff edge.

I realised I hadn't spoken for a while and I didn't want her to leave this odd situation without having said anything. 'I hope the funeral goes well tomorrow,' I blurted out after her.

She stopped and turned, looking at us through her sunglasses. 'I'll see you there.'

I didn't understand. 'What? How do you mean?'

'I mean, I want you to come to the funeral. Both of you,' she clarified, nodding at Noah. 'If he's not too young.'

'I'm not too young, I'm seventeen,' he answered. I still wasn't sure how appropriate it was, but I knew he wouldn't take no for an answer now he'd been invited.

'Yes of course, we both knew him a little,' I said. 'We'll come along and pay our respects.'

'That's very kind, Edward, but not just that. I need your help. I'll talk to you more after the funeral, but I have a job for you. You need to prove that my husband was murdered.'

Not giving me time to reply, she simply turned and began her descent down the cliff back towards the village.

4

'Okay, let's look out for people acting suspiciously.'

'They're grieving, Noah,' I whispered back. 'People act in all sorts of ways. But we should respect their privacy.'

We were at the funeral. I'd thought of not attending but Noah wouldn't hear of it once Mary had invited us, especially as Chalk Gap Church was just across the square from us: although that had meant Noah wasn't the only person tagging along.

'Funeral are public, love, it's fair game if you ask me. If anyone acts suspiciously, they've probably got something to hide.'

'Mum, I'm not even sure why you're here. You didn't even really know Jackson.' Jackson and Mary had moved out of the village a few years ago, now living in nearby Seaford.

'Edward, don't be so rude! I watched him grow up and I know his mother. And we're doing the wake, it's right that I represent the pub and show our respects.'

I wasn't entirely sure how much respect she

was showing at that moment, as we were halfway through the service and she wasn't even bothering to whisper. 'Mum, ssshh!'

'I don't know what's up with you,' she 'whispered' back, marginally lower than her original volume. 'You're here to look at your suspects, it's the perfect time.'

'Exactly!' Noah said, taking his phone out ready to make notes. 'Let's have a look at who we've got.'

'As far as we know, it was ruled a suicide,' I reminded of them. 'I just want to be respectful to Mary King and hear what she's got to say.'

'Stop spoiling the fun, Edward. I know the family, by sight, I'll tell you,' Mum said, directing her last words to Noah.

I sighed to myself; she was going to do this anyway and it would be good to know about the family before speaking to Mary. 'Fine, Mum, just make sure you whisper.'

'What do you think I'm doing?' she said, looking at me incredulously, before continuing at the same volume. 'Okay, so front bench on our side. Obviously, you've got Annabelle King, his mother.'

I looked over at the back of the lady in her sixties at the front of where we were. Three women about her age were reaching forward to comfort her from the bench behind – family members, maybe – but she remained alone in the front bench. They'd seemed to have observed 'sides' of the church, like a wedding, and I immediately noticed that the King family side had more people. According to Mum, the Kings had always been a church-going family, so it made sense.

Annabelle King herself was dressed all in black, like everyone else, and I could only see the back of her head right now, but I knew her anyway from running our local shop. She'd managed it as long as I could remember, and she was the kind of formidable lady everyone was a little scared of, with a terrifying tone to her voice which scared off shoplifters and shoppers alike.

'I think she's crying,' Noah said. 'I wonder what that means for our investigation.'

'I've no idea how you can tell from there,' I commented, doubting that this human dragon of a woman would cry in public, even at her son's death. 'But if she is, it means she's grieving for her son.'

'Then there's her other son, I can't believe he's shown his face,' Mum continued, turning her head to point out a man sat alone at the back of the church. 'I thought it was him when we walked past him, I barely recognised him though after all these years.' Most people probably wouldn't have recognised him, but Mum doesn't miss a trick.

I only knew Jackson himself vaguely growing up, being a couple of years above me at school, but his brother was three or four years older still and I couldn't even remember his name. Not that I'd recognise him from his appearance today: his head was down, he had stubble that was almost a beard, and wore dark sunglasses: presumably to shield his eyes from the bright February sun the late winter's day had graced us with, but I didn't know why he hadn't took them off inside.

'Jonny King, that's him, look at him in his shades. Probably doesn't want people to know he's turned up,' Mum said, as if reading my mind. 'Black sheep of the family he is. Annabelle's not seen him for years. Not after what happened.'

'What happened?' Noah asked, falling for Mum's trick of leaving unfinished gossip dangling.

'It was a good ten years or so ago now, but Mary, Jackson's wife, was Jonny's girlfriend first.'

'Did they have an affair?' Noah asked, with excitement. The lady in the bench in front of turned round and glared at him.

'No, not as far as I know,' Mum said, returning the lady's glare but lowering her voice. 'Jonny and Mary had broken up the year before, quite a bad break up, by all accounts. Jonny had left the village, but Jackson and Mary were still in it, and you can guess what that led to.'

The lady in front turned again, this time giving a dirty look to Mum. 'Will you have some respect?'

'Yes, of course, sorry, I'll whisper,' Mum replied, smiling her fakest smile and not really getting the woman's point. 'Anyway, obviously Jonny didn't take it very well, I mean, you wouldn't, would you?

But what he did, he went too far. No one deserves that.'

'What did he do?' Noah asked, hanging on her every word. I suddenly remembered where the story was heading. Of course, the two warring brothers. I'd forgotten it was the Kings.

'Jonny beat him up,' Mum whispered dramatically. 'Jackson ended up in hospital.'

'No!' Noah chimed, giving Mum the shocked reaction I knew she wanted.

'Oh yes,' she continued, 'He beat him black and blue. I don't think Jackson ever got over it, at least not psychologically. Most people think that's what started his *mental health problems*.' She mouthed these last three words, almost silently.

'Remind me what happened after that?' I asked, cursing myself for joining in.

'Annabelle and the rest of the family sided with Jackson, disowned him. Jonny was arrested but I think they agreed not to press charges if he stayed out of the way.'

'But he's not out of the way now, he's right there,' Noah pointed out, somewhat needlessly.

'Of course he's going to pay respects to his brother,' I said, glancing back over at Jonny.

'Is Jackson and Jonny's dad around?' was Noah's next question, which he obviously didn't ask quietly enough, as the lady in front once again turned round.

'Who, Fozzy? He hasn't been around since the boys were young kids.'

Noah and I both looked puzzled as she continued. 'That's what he was known as, I can't even remember his first name, he was always just Fozzy round here. They were never married either; King is Annabelle's name and she always kept it for her and the boys.'

Long gone,' she added, before glancing over to the front bench on the opposite side of the church. 'Then you've got Mary and her family on the other side. I don't really know Mary, her and Jackson kept themselves to themselves, even before they left the village. But her sister, Terri, next to her, she works in the shop for Annabelle. Quiet girl she is. And do you know, Annabelle had both of them back in the shop the very next day? Her own son and Terri's brother-in-law, but she still opened the shop. Make of that what you will.'

I looked over and recognised both sisters from my behind diagonal view, with an older man and woman who were presumably their parents with them; Mary's mum was carrying a baby, which must have been Jackson and Mary's baby son. I knew Terri from my visits to the village shop; each time I visited, I crossed my fingers that she would be the one serving me in her shy, pleasant manner, rather than the blunt, bolshy Annabelle.

As I contemplated this, I noticed Mary stand up and move to the front of the church as Reverend

Flowers called her name to speak about her husband.

The whole church was in silence, waiting, as she approached the lectern. Even Mum and Noah had stopped talking. As she looked out on us, I noticed two things: she had no notes or script with her, and she looked determined.

'Thank you to everyone here for coming to pay their respects to my husband, and for all the messages, thoughts and wishes over the last couple of weeks. It shows what a wonderful man Jackson was, and how many people loved him. He was an incredible husband.'

'You'd think she'd mention him being a father too,' Mum whispered. I nudged her to be quiet as Mary continued.

'I know many of you have said that the silver lining of Jackson's death is that it can raise mental health awareness. And I appreciate that so much. Jackson did suffer with poor mental health, quite badly, and in fighting it he was the bravest man I ever knew. But…'

She paused for breath, and I felt goosebumps in my embarrassment of what she might say next.

'Here we go,' Mum whispered, nudging me.

'But,' Mary continued, looking out round the congregation, 'it isn't a fight that he would have given up on. I just know he wouldn't. So, I don't care what the coroner says. My husband did not commit suicide.'

There was a collective gasp throughout the church. Annabelle King stood up. Knowing her no nonsense personality, I expected a showdown. But she simply said quietly, barely audible, 'Mary, please, no. Don't do this. Not today.'

'I'm sorry, Annabelle, I'm not trying to cause a scene on purpose. I know he was your son, but he was my husband. And I know he wouldn't kill himself. He was murdered.' The shocked noises raced round the room again, all eyes glued to the floor show. But Mary wasn't done. 'And Edward Crisp is going to prove it.'

Wait, what? I was nervous enough already, simply on Mary's behalf, watching the drama unfold. But I wasn't expecting to be named as a lead player in that drama.

The lady in front spun round. '*That's* why you've been talking all through the service, you're here to poke your nose in. Why don't you let him rest in peace?' I didn't even know this lady, but she clearly knew who I was.

'My Edward's just doing as he's been asked by Mary, why don't *you* leave him alone?' my mum retorted. However, it wasn't just the lady in front anymore; everyone in the church was now looking at me.

But that didn't last long, as we heard Mary's voice booming from the lectern once more. 'That's him, that's the murderer! Go on, run, you coward! Like you did when you killed my husband, your own brother!'

We all turned to see Jonny King fleeing the church.

5

‘How dare you turn my son’s funeral into a circus like this? As if you’ve not done enough already!’ Annabelle screamed now at Mary, moving closer to the lectern.

‘Why was *he* even here?’ Mary screamed back. ‘He put him there, can’t we just bury him in peace?’

‘Ladies, that is ENOUGH!’ Reverend Flowers boomed in his authoritative voice, silencing them immediately. I was surprised the Reverend had let it get that far. ‘I will not have this behaviour in my church. Now, can you both sit down, and can we bury *your* husband and *your* son with the respect he deserves. Please.’ That last word was more gentle and sympathetic in tone, as if he remembered he was dealing with two grieving women, something I knew he understood.

The rest of the church service passed without incident, though I knew that this wasn’t the end of it.

So did Mum, who was the first person out of the church, not even staying for the burial. ‘I better go and make sure your Dad and Alfie have got everything ready. Everyone’s gonna come into the pub to see round two, it'll be standing room only. I can't wait!'

The burial was also event free, but it was extremely sad. The finality of it hit me as I watched the coffin going into the ground: Jackson was only a couple of years older than me and this was the end of his life.

I contemplated this for a few moments alone in the graveyard, leaving everyone else to head across the village square to the pub, including Noah who was keen to 'interview key witnesses.'

Before I knew it, I found myself visiting the graves of each of the victims of the four murders I'd solved. When I arrived at the last one, closest to the Vicarage house, I found the Vicar himself.

'Sorry, Reverend Flowers, I didn't mean to disturb you.'

'It's okay, Edward,' he said as he smiled at me. 'It's a funny thing, isn't it, death?'

I didn't quite know how to reply; I wasn't sure if he was expecting a spiritual conversation about it.

He must have seen the panic on my face. 'It's alright, Edward, don't worry. I just mean none of us ever know when it's coming.'

'Do you think Jackson did?' I asked that question before I could stop myself.

'I think he did, yes,' Flowers answered slowly, looking at me. 'I think he must have been in a great deal of pain.'

I knew what he was implying, but before I had chance to query it, he carried on. 'I wish I could give Mary King the answers she wants, but I can't. And neither can you, Edward.'

'I know, I'm not trying to.' Wasn't I? Mary hadn't given me time on the clifftop to refuse or even discuss her request, and had then mentioned me in her outlandish assertion, when all I'd done by that point was attend the funeral. But what if this was more than grieving denial? 'You don't think there's any chance it could be murder, Vicar?'

'I don't *think* Edward, I *know* there's no chance, I'm afraid. It definitely wasn't murder; one of my Chaplains witnessed it.'

6

Of course. One of the many great things Reverend Flowers has done for Chalk Gap is create a search and rescue Chaplaincy volunteer team, to patrol the East and West Chalk Cliffs either side of the village, reaching out and offering support to anyone they find up there who might be in distress.

Nearby Beachy Head has had a Chaplaincy team for many years, which is very effective, but doesn't stretch as far as the two Chalk Gap cliffs. On learning this on his arrival a few years ago, Flowers worked with BHCT, using their expertise to help him train his own team along the same lines.

'What happened, Reverend?'

'Our volunteers do work their shifts in pairs, you understand,' he started, as if explaining himself. 'But we have a limited number of volunteers, and the daytime shifts are less likely to find anyone in any distress. So, from time to time, when we are short staffed, the two volunteers would take a cliff each, East Chalk and West Chalk, and use our radio system to communicate.'

I saw where this was going. 'And that's what happened on the day Jackson was up there.'

'Yes, though I don't think it would have made a difference, sadly. From what I understand, it all happened so quickly that Nathan didn't stand a chance of saving him.'

'Nathan, that was the Chaplain on duty?'

'Yes, the poor soul.'

'And he saw Jackson jump?'

The Reverend nodded this time.

'Did he manage to speak to him, what happened?'

'Obviously, we have procedures to follow, when we are reaching out to the despondent.' He seemed to want to emphasise that his team were following all the correct procedures, but I didn't doubt that; if they were trained by the BHCT I knew they would be, as they had an excellent reputation. 'But with Jackson, there wasn't time. Nathan tried to engage him from a safe distance, but he barely listened. He just jumped.'

This made no sense. Mary King must have known about this witness; how could she still think it was murder? Although we still only had one man's word for it.

Reverend Flowers must have known what I was thinking in the long silence after he spoke. 'All of our Chaplains are carefully vetted, including ID checks and references from their parish if they're not from mine.'

'Oh, I thought all the volunteers must be villagers.'

'Most are, but not necessarily. Some just prefer to volunteer in a smaller remit, rather than Beachy Head. Nathan, for example, lives in Eastbourne. I had a lovely letter from his parish Vicar.'

I thought of the poor man who had witnessed this terrible incident. 'How is Nathan now?'

'He's doing okay, but he's had a couple of weeks off with anxiety. I went to see him last week, I'm going again tomorrow. He put on a brave face but, to be honest, I'm not sure he'll come back.'

The Reverend looked sadly at the gravestone as he spoke these words. He was right: death was a funny thing. I wasn't sure if I'd be able to return if I'd witnessed that.

'What do you think I should do about Mary King?' I asked. 'She wants me to investigate.'

'You'll find the right words, Edward, you always seem to.' I blushed at the compliment. 'If you like, tell her you've spoken to me and you've heard about the witness, I don't mind.'

'Yes, it's strange she didn't tell me that herself,' I mused.

'It's her way of coping, I expect. And though I don't know Jackson's brother, it's before my time, it sounds like he's an easy person to lash out at, based on their history.'

'Thank you, Reverend,' I said, considering offering my hand to shake but instead settling on an awkward smile. 'I just hope she'll accept that Jackson wasn't murdered.'

7

'Of course he was murdered!'

'Noah, how do you explain that? There's a witness to his death.'

I'd returned to the pub too late for the wake, which apparently had been a bit of a damp squib, much to Mum's disappointment ('barely lasted half an hour, and everyone on soft drinks, waste of our time! And not even a raised voice, they're no fun.').

Noah, however, was in his element discussing the twists and turns of the case. 'I still think it's murder, the Chaplain witness just makes it more of a puzzle for us: an impossible mystery. Don't worry, I've read lots of mysteries like that, I'll help you solve it.'

I let out a loud sigh as I tried to avoid replying rudely. Noah meant well, and we did share a love of murder mysteries, but his tendency to imagine that we're in one could be exasperating at times. 'Noah, I just think Mary is very upset and is clinging on to any hope that her husband didn't take his own life.'

'Maybe, but you can ask her anyway.'

'What do you mean?' I asked.

'She's here now, so you can talk to her about it,' he beamed and nodded his head towards Mary, who had just arrived at our table.

'Talk to me about what?' she asked, looking flustered. 'Actually, never mind, I need to talk to you anyway. You need to help me prove that Jonny murdered Jackson.'

'Mary, take a seat,' I said, in my most gentle voice. 'Noah, I was meant to help Mum clear the buffet away, can you go and help her for me so I can have a chat with Mary?'

He looked like he was about to protest, but didn't. 'Oh, okay, of course,' he said, as he sauntered away sadly.

'You should have let him stay,' she said as she settled into her chair. 'I think he's the only one who believes me.'

'It's not that I don't believe you, Mary.'

'I went back to Jackson's grave and I saw you with Reverend Flowers. I can guess what you were talking about but it doesn't change anything for me.' She looked straight at me, but it didn't seem confrontational: just matter-of-fact and direct. I didn't understand her, but I decided then that I liked Mary; even if she was wrong, she had courage in her convictions and I admired her for it.

'Mary, how can it possibly be murder when there's a witness to what happened?'

'I don't know,' she snapped before going silent. As

the seconds passed and I saw the pain in her expression, I decided something.

'Okay, if I was to play along, hypothetically, and consider that this could have been murder, I'd need you to be completely open and honest with me.'

Her face lit up as she nodded. 'Absolutely.'

'Even if the questions are difficult for you to answer.' I wasn't sure of this one myself; asking personal, potentially upsetting, questions was probably my least favourite part of my new found amateur detective life in recent months.

'Of course,' she said, though I thought I saw her flinch. Her husband's mental health and death were not going to be easy topics. But I'd wait to come on to them.

'Why are you so sure that Jackson's brother killed him? Did you think it was him when you first mentioned murder to me, even before you saw him in church?'

'Great first question. Or should I say, questions,' she said. 'I know it sounds crazy, which is why I've asked you and not the police. I've no proof. In fact, as you just said, it doesn't even seem possible due to the chaplain's account. But, do you know when you just *know*? Have you ever just known something in your gut, without knowing how or why, but you just *know*?'

I thought for a moment. I'd solved the murders I had so far with a combination of logic, evidence, and, yes, I guess, gut reaction. But you have to have the first two along with it or else you won't get very far. I told her this.

'That's where you come in,' she said. 'I know it; I need you to prove it. But I haven't answered your question properly yet. Apart from my gut, how do I know? Two reasons. My husband would never go through with killing himself, for one. And two, he has a brother who hates him, who's capable of anything.'

I wasn't going to get to the bottom of this without asking difficult questions. 'You were in a relationship with Jonny before Jackson, weren't you?'

She frowned and paused, and I noticed her drumming her fingers on the table rapidly. It occurred to me that I should have offered her a drink.

'It was a long time ago but yes, I was. It's funny how something can be both the worst and best thing that happened to you. It was the worst time of my life, with that evil man, but without that experience I'd never have met his brother: the best man I ever knew.'

'In what ways was Jonny evil?' Another question that wouldn't be easy for her to answer.

'I'm sure you know about him putting Jackson in hospital; that gives you an idea what he's capable of. But violence wasn't the problem when he was with me, at least not physical. He was a manipulative control freak. He had to know where I was at all times, who I was with; he even tried to stop me seeing my sister, let alone any friends.'

It sounded awful. As you might know, I don't have much experience with relationships, but I still knew that often what we see in public is very different to behind closed doors. 'I'm sorry to hear that. What happened at the end?'

'I broke up with him and he wouldn't leave me alone. Contacting me and following me everywhere, and in this village you can't escape someone like that. His mum practically forced him to move to Eastbourne, even rented a room there for him. Annabelle and Jackson knew what he was like. They were a brilliant support, actually; that's how I became close to Jackson.'

I was starting to see how things had unfolded. 'Have you or Jackson see Jonny at all after the attack?'

'No, not for ten years.'

I looked at her and she looked away for a second; I wasn't convinced she was being completely honest. 'Really? Not at all?'

She was quiet for a moment before she spoke again. 'Okay, there was one time. One day early last year, Jackson and I were shopping in Eastbourne. We saw Jonny in *Boots* in the Arndale Centre.'

Silence again. I was expecting another part of the story. 'And?' I asked gently.

'And nothing,' she replied defensively. 'We ignored him, he stared after us for a minute, and that was it.'

Again, I could tell this wasn't the full story. Something occurred to me; Boots was a Pharmacy, and as we were now in February, early last year was probably a year or so ago at the most. I tried to do some quick maths in my head. 'Remind me, how old is Joshua?'

She laughed out loud. 'I knew there was a reason I asked you to help, looks like you're as smart as they say you are. He's nearly five months old, and yes, we were buying a pregnancy test.'

'And Jonny saw you?'

'Yes,' she said quickly, as she rolled her eyes. 'It's funny, Jackson didn't want to go to the village pharmacy to get it in case anyone saw us, so we went to Eastbourne and bumped straight into his brother.'

'And was that the end of it?'

She sighed and glanced across the nearly empty pub. 'As I'm sure you've guessed, no it wasn't. He got in touch with Annabelle and let her know she'd be a grandma before we'd even told her ourselves. Then, he kept trying to contact Jackson, saying he wanted to be involved as an uncle.

'But he didn't contact you?'

'No, he didn't.'

'And, just to check, he saw you buying the test, and the next you'd heard he'd contacted his mum? He didn't do anything else in between?'

'No, that's it,' she said, eyeing me suspiciously.

Then how did he know that Annabelle was definitely going to be a grandma, I thought to myself.

8

'Why now?' I asked. 'All of this is so long ago, even when you bumped into him is over a year ago. Why would he target Jackson now?'

'I wasn't sure of that myself until recently,' she replied. 'But I managed to get some info out of my sister about Annabelle. She's been back in touch with Jonny the last couple of months, without telling us. But a week before Jackson's death, she decided it wasn't fair to Jackson and cut it off. I guess Jonny wasn't too happy with it.'

I thought of the situation Annabelle was in. No matter what Jonny had done, he was her son and now the only one she had left. 'Have you spoken to Annabelle about this?'

She smiled knowingly. 'Me and Annabelle aren't exactly on speaking terms.'

'Okay, so what do you want me to do?'

'Find out what happened. Maybe Reverend Flowers will let you speak to this Chaplain witness. I tried and he wouldn't let me, for obvious reasons. But we have to find him and get his story ourselves. He must be mistaken, or he's someone Jonny knows and he's got him to lie.'

'Reverend Flowers says the Chaplains are carefully ID'd and vetted.'

'And then there's the school,' she continued, ignoring my reply. 'This business about them receiving a hand-delivered note, which they've denied. You need to talk to them too.'

'Mary, I'm not sure.' The story of the note left at the school was certainly intriguing, but I still couldn't see how it was possible for a murder to have been committed. I did feel sorry for her though, and she seemed determined. But there was one more thing bothering me, and I was trying to work out how to say it.

'I really hope I word this right and I hope it doesn't upset you further. But I just wanted to know a little about Jackson's mental health, after you mentioned it in church.'

She met my gaze head on. 'Yes, I expected you to ask me that. Lots of people think that it proves it was suicide. But I know Jackson and he wouldn't have. Yes, he'd had thoughts and been close to it, but, ultimately, he was never able to go through with it.'

'Was he diagnosed with anything?'

'Eventually. Doctor Albright is a brilliant GP but it's so tough getting referred to community mental health. Every time she referred him, he'd have an initial phone call with a mental health nurse who was kind of like a gatekeeper to their services. It's not their fault, the service is so stretched, but he kept getting knocked back to the GP. As soon as they heard he was a teacher it's like he wasn't crazy enough.'

I knew the feeling; I'd struggled to get support with my own mental health, but Doctor Albright had always been a great help. 'Did he finally get to meet a psychiatrist?'

She sighed deeply. 'After a couple of A&E visits once things got really bad. In the end, he was diagnosed with PTSD.'

Post-traumatic Stress Disorder, it made sense after his brother's attack years ago. 'Do you think that was the right diagnosis?'

'It all started after Jonny attacked him, so it makes sense.' She paused. 'Look, Edward. I know what it looks like. You'd struggle to find anyone who doesn't think it's suicide. But I just know. Please. Speak to the chaplain witness and the school, and if nothing comes of either, I promise I'll drop it.'

I'm not great at saying no to people, and I soon found myself replying with the answer she wanted. 'Okay, I'll do it.'

She looked visibly relieved. 'Thank you, Edward, thank you so much.'

I wasn't sure she'd have much to thank me for, but I hoped I could help her accept her husband's death, whatever the cause.

9

'I'm so excited that we're on the way to investigate a murder! I wonder what we'll find out!'

'Noah, Jackson's death was a very sad tragedy, and I hope we can help Mary come to terms with it, but we can't treat this like a murder – because it isn't.' You're probably thinking that was me telling Noah off, but it wasn't.

'Okay, sorry Reverend,' he replied from the back seat of the car.

I'd managed to persuade Reverend Flowers to let me and Noah tag along the next day on his visit to Eastbourne to see Nathan, the Chaplain who was there at the end with Jackson. He'd also reluctantly agreed to take us to Jackson's last school while we were in the area (as a non-driver, I realised it would be difficult to be an amateur detective full-time).

'Edward, I hope you know what you're doing. I have every sympathy for Mary, but there is nothing more to Jackson's death than we already know.'

'But what if there is?' Noah asked the Reverend. '*The Mystery of Jackson King* still needs to be solved.'

'Sorry what?' Reverend Flowers asked as he tried

to concentrate on the road ahead.

'Noah kind of names each of our 'cases', as if they were mystery novels,' I explained.

I heard Flowers exhale deeply as he turned his car left into Eastbourne's Old Town area. 'I'm starting to wonder if this was a good idea, Edward. We can't upset Nathan, he's been through enough. All three of us together might be a bit much for him.'

I knew where this was going. Luckily, Noah wasn't listening. 'Oh look, Old Town Community Library! Pull up for a second, Reverend. I love it here, I used to go all the time when we lived in Eastbourne. In fact, there's a book I wanted to see if I could get from here.'

The Reverend and I smiled at each other. 'Noah, how about you go in the library and I'll go with the Reverend to see Nathan? Then we can get you on the way back and we'll all go to the school together.'

I turned my head to see Noah looking conflicted. He clearly wanted to join in with the visit but I knew the allure of the library would be too much. 'Okay, I'll go to the library. But you'll update me on everything that happens?'

'Of course.' I smiled and then felt a pang of guilt in excluding him. And also for the Library Manager, Kate, a good acquaintance of mine who I liaised with frequently as the nearest community library to our school. She was lovely and very helpful, but I already imagined the dozens of questions that Noah would throw at the poor lady. 'Say hello to Kate from me but she will be busy, so just have a quick chat, then let her get on with her work.'

'Oh, she might need me to give her some help then! I'll ask her,' he said cheerily as he got out of the car, before I could protest.

'Thank you, Edward,' Reverend Flowers said as we drove off. 'I know Noah means well, but I don't want to alarm Nathan too much. I don't think he'll mind you being there, but Noah too might have added to his anxiety a little.'

I understood completely. I'd had the same dilemma each time Noah had helped me in one of these cases; he enjoyed playing detective, and he actually could be quite helpful, but sometimes his manner might take a little getting used to.

My thoughts moved to Nathan, as we turned off the main road into the estate he lived on. Was there any possibility at all he was mistaken, or even lying? Reverend Flowers was insistent that he'd been properly verified and was of good character. Mary seemed to think that Jonny had managed to get to him somehow, or he was a friend who had been put up to it, but it seemed unlikely.

As we arrived at Nathan's doorstep and I immediately saw how anxious he was, my immediate reaction was that it was unfair for me to be there; I should have let Mary down gently and not got myself into this. He was clean shaven, so was at least looking after himself, but otherwise the man looked tired and withdrawn.

Nathan's house looked lovely from the outside; it was a large semi-detached house on a pleasant looking street, and I knew that Old Town was one of the nicest areas of Eastbourne. But as he led us into what I thought was the living room, I noticed that this was a shabby-looking studio bedroom.

'I live in a house share,' he muttered to me, likely registering the look on my face, as I became conscious that Reverend Flowers hadn't introduced us yet.

'Me too,' I offered back. 'It looks nice.' I compared Nathan's situation to my own, sharing a house with my best friend Patrick (and previously our friend Kat). It certainly helped my mental health not living on my own, and maybe it was the same for him.

'This is Edward, a friend of mine,' the Reverend said as he gestured towards me. 'I hope you don't mind me bringing him. Edward has suffered with anxiety too, and has overcome it really well. I thought it might be helpful for you to meet him.'

I didn't know this was the cover story Reverend Flowers was going with. Then I realised, that for the Reverend, it probably wasn't just a cover story. He was a very honest, kind man and this was probably the reason he'd used to justify to himself bringing me.

Nathan considered me for a moment, with an unconvincing smile plastered on his face. He looked like he was about to say something different, but instead he settled on, 'Hello, Edward.'

'Nice to meet you,' I replied. 'And I'm sorry about what you witnessed with Jackson like that. It must have been difficult.'

He looked surprised that I'd mentioned Jackson directly; maybe I'd done it too soon. I resolved to let the Reverend lead the rest of the conversation as Nathan ignored my comment and offered us a seat. We both sat down on the sofa, the only place to sit in the room other than the bed, which Nathan placed himself on.

'How have you been doing, Nathan?' Reverend Flowers asked as his volunteer hovered uncomfortably on the bed opposite us.

'I've been doing okay,' he replied, without looking at either of us. 'But I've made a decision, Reverend. I'm afraid I'm not going to continue with the Chaplain work.'

'Ah, I'm sorry,' the Reverend said back gently. 'I thought you might say that. I'm sad to see you go, but you must put your own well-being first.'

'I thought I'd be able to handle it,' Nathan mumbled, while still looking at the floor. 'But I can't. I still see him. Every night, pretty much. I see him step forward into nothing and drop; I replay our conversation in my head.'

Reverend Flowers leaned forward and put his hand on Nathan's knee. 'You did everything you could. This isn't your fault.'

Nathan blinked hard as if he was trying to hold off

tears. 'I keep hearing his last words to me.'

'What were they?' I coaxed, speaking before I realised that maybe I shouldn't.

'*Tell Mary I love her.* I think Mary was his wife. It was the only time he mentioned her, but I read her name in the papers.'

This was interesting, and the first time I'd heard it; Mary hadn't told me this, but I supposed it was painful and personal. I remembered the role I'd been introduced under before I continued. 'I'm so sorry, it must have been awful for you. You haven't met his wife, then? Maybe it would help you to move on.'

He looked up and set his eyes on mine. 'I'm afraid not. I know she wanted to, but I just couldn't face it. I didn't know what I'd say to her. I've thought about her though, I hope she's okay.'

'She's okay,' the Reverend reassured him. 'We had the funeral yesterday.'

'Of course,' Nathan replied. 'I should have gone, but I couldn't face it.'

'Nathan,' Reverend Flowers said in his gentle, kind manner. 'Don't let this define you. You became a Chaplain volunteer because you wanted to do good. You'll find another way to do it, I know you will.'

'Thank you, Reverend,' he said as he smiled weakly. 'Yes, I hope so. I just wanted to prevent suffering if I could.'

This made me think of something I wanted to

know; many people volunteer for roles like that after suffering a tragedy of their own. 'If you don't mind me asking, what made you want to be a search and rescue Chaplain?'

Again, he looked a little shocked by the question, but answered easily enough. 'A friend of mine took his own life at your village cliffs last year and I wanted to stop other people doing that if I could.'

Reverend Flowers nodded along, obviously knowing this already from Nathan's recruitment. 'I think some fund-raising for mental health charities might be a nice thing to do for your friend instead. I'll send you some links when I get home.'

'Thank you, Reverend, and thank you both for coming to see me.' He stood up from the bed as he said this, signifying that it was time for us to go.'

As he saw us to the door, I thought of the short conversation we'd had with him. I couldn't put my finger on it, but something didn't feel right. That's why I asked the question I did on the doorstep.

'I'm sorry to ask, but just to check, you don't happen to know Jackson's brother, do you? Jonny King?'

'No, I don't,' he replied immediately. But I knew from his face that he definitely did.

10

We were in the car outside the library waiting for Noah, and Reverend Flowers was not happy with me. 'I knew I shouldn't have let you come with me. You had no right to mention Jonny King like that.'

'If he doesn't know him, and he's nothing to hide, it doesn't matter, he wouldn't have minded,' I countered. I was now certain that Nathan was hiding something.

'It was an odd question to say the least, Edward. I think you've been spending a little too much time with young Noah.'

'Come on, Reverend, I know all the murder mysteries I read aren't real; I'm usually just as cynical myself about stuff like this. But the way he flinched when I said Jonny King's name, something wasn't right. He definitely knows him. And we only have his word for it that he was actually up there in the first place.' Upon seeing the Reverend's face, I knew I'd gone too far.

'For God's sake, Edward,' he said, raising his voice, in a rare moment of blasphemy as he picked up his mobile phone. 'Nathan is a good man, an honest man. Look at this.'

He thrusted his mobile phone into my hand, with the device open on a photo of a document. 'What's this?'

'I keep all my Chaplains' references and ID backed up in a secure folder on my phone, just in case. Read it.'

I looked at the phone as I grinned to myself at the thought of probably the most technologically advanced Vicar in East Sussex. In front of me was a screenshot of an email from a Reverend File in Eastbourne, confirming that Nathan had been attending his church for around ten years and was a good member of the congregation, who volunteered for many fund-raising activities.

'And before you ask, the email isn't forged, and I know Reverend File personally. He's a photoshop whizz and he always helps me with my advertising for our church events.'

As I marvelled yet again at the IT abilities of our local clergymen, Reverend Flowers continued. 'In fact, I had a chat on the phone with him about Nathan, he sang his praises. Now scroll to the next photo.'

In front of me now was a picture of Nathan's driving license, with his name *Nathan Foster* and photograph clearly displayed. There was no doubt this man's ID and references checked out.

'I trust him, Edward,' Reverend Flowers said solemnly as he took the phone back from me. ‘So should you.’

I was saved from replying by my own phone ringing, though I was surprised by the name I saw on the screen: Noah.

‘Hello!’ he said loudly and brightly, not sounding remotely like he was in a library.

‘Noah, where are you? We’re waiting outside the library for you.’

‘Oh I’m not there,’ he replied cheerfully. ‘I finished up at the library, so I walked over to the school to query about the note.’

Oh no. ‘You did what? You haven’t actually spoken to anyone have you?’

‘Oh yes, they’ve been very helpful.’

This sounded like a disaster; I could barely imagine how Noah would have handled this sensitive case with Jackson’s last employers. ‘Stay there, Noah, we’re on our way.’

11

I doubt any man of the cloth had ever driven faster than Reverend Flowers drove across Eastbourne to Noah's location.

'Edward, we are out of our depth. We need to get Noah and leave this whole situation alone.'

The Reverend wasn't used to the rollercoaster ride that was an amateur investigation with Noah, though I still wasn't sure I was.

'I'm sure it will be fine,' I reassured him as we got out of his car in the school car park.

'Then why is Mr. Molyneux waiting outside reception for us with Noah?' Flowers asked as he gestured towards where Noah stood waving, accompanied by a tall middle-aged, balding man who I vaguely recognised as the Head Teacher.

'Reverend Flowers!' he said loudly across the car park as I tried to decipher his tone. 'It's been a long time.'

We reached him and he shook our hands warmly in turn, before patting Noah on the shoulder. 'This young man's explained everything about why you're here.'

Oh, has he?' Reverend Flowers replied with clear trepidation in his voice. 'What did he tell you exactly?'

'Just that you're here on behalf of the church Jackson belonged to, and you wanted to have a chat with us about him. This is a fine young man you have representing your parish.'

'Thank you, Mr Molyneux,' Noah said as he beamed. 'Yes, I've been telling him all about our investigation, and that we need to know all about this mysterious letter that was left for Mr King.'

'Noah, if you go back inside to Judy at reception, she'll take you to the school library for your tour. They'll be ready for you now.'

Noah bounded off with delight, as the smile on Mr Molyneux's face dropped suddenly. He instantly looked much older and very worried. 'You must be Edward Crisp.'

Listen, Mike, I can explain -' Reverend Flowers started.

'No, Allan. I'm the one who needs to explain. I've been expecting someone to come about this letter business for weeks. I'm just glad it's you two and not the press or the police.' He shivered a little in his suit, which made me wonder why we were conducting this conversation in the car park rather than inside. He turned to me. 'I know you by the way, Edward. You're the one who solved the murders in your village: Miss Finch and the snow day ones. Sorry again to hear about that, Allan.'

I tried to move the conversation on quickly. 'So, there was a letter left for Jackson then?'

'No, well, maybe.' He looked utterly perplexed as he paused. 'The thing is, we don't think so. But we don't know for certain.'

'Mike, what's going on?' the Reverend asked.

'Let me start by saying that Jackson, even though with for a short time, was a valued member of our school family and we are all deeply sad to lose him.' I was starting to wonder if he thought we *were* the press. 'If there is more to the story of what happened to him, I want to help in any way I can, regardless of any trouble the school gets into.'

I'm adept at identifying when someone is nervous, and I could tell this man needed bringing to the point. 'It's okay, Mr Molyneux. Just tell us what happened in your own time.'

'Our school prides itself in our student ambassadors,' he started, seemingly still not ready to get to the point quite yet. 'And largely, this is a system that works very well. All of our students, of all ages and abilities on a rota system, get turns undertaking various duties throughout the day. One of those duties is our internal post system.'

I saw where this was going.

'Judy does a great job overseeing the students doing this, of course, but it isn't an infallible system. The day of Jackson's... erm, on Jackson's last day with us, the student on post duty that day was a particularly enthusiastic helper. Maybe a little *too* enthusiastic, but at our school we encourage our students to be individuals and embrace their personality: not to be afraid to speak out.'

I thought of the kindly way he addressed Noah a few moments ago. 'That seems a great way to run a school. What happened with the post helper that day, though?'

He rubbed his arms on his shoulders, and I couldn't tell if this was through cold or nerves. 'She did all her post duties just fine. Judy gives them the pile to sort out and they just get on with it, she doesn't know exactly what's in there. Obviously, the tragedy with Jackson happened that day, and over the next couple of days the story was everywhere – the news, social media and the rest of it. Which is when a rumour started spreading round school: one that we were able to trace back to our post helper that day.'

I noted that he hadn't told us her name and, due to safeguarding and data protection, wasn't likely to. 'This rumour being that she had a hand delivered letter for Jackson in her post pile, and delivered it to him in class?'

'Precisely. And you know what it's like; students speak to their parents, parents speak to their friends, and before you know it, it's all over everywhere that Jackson received a letter here that day.'

'And did you manage to get to the bottom of it?' Reverend Flowers asked.

'In a way. Unfortunately, the student concerned does have a history of making up tall tales. When we spoke to her, she backtracked and said she might be mistaken. And we can find no other evidence of it. Judy didn't see anyone drop anything off, but that's not to say they didn't when she had her back turned. Members of Jackson's class remember the post helper dropping the post off, but standard messages go to each teacher every day, and we found a couple of those left on the desk in his classroom.'

'But not the mystery letter, which he could have taken with him.'

'Exactly. Gentlemen, the whole thing is such a mess. I've been quite worried about it. I did ring up and spoke to someone in CID, a DI Appleby, but he told me not to worry about it. He said he'd send someone to speak to me, but they never came.'

I rolled my eyes at the mention of my old frenemy, who clearly thought this was suicide, end of story. 'No, you did everything you could, and you've told us now, so don't worry any more.'

'What will happen next?'

I thought about that for a moment. I came into this out of sympathy with Mary King and not much else; I never expected there to be any substance to her claims. Now, I had no idea.

12

We arrived back in Chalk Gap to a one-woman welcoming committee. We'd barely stepped out of the car when Annabelle King came flying over to us.

'I want a word with you two!'

'But there's three of us,' Noah stated as she shot him a look of utter disdain.

'What's this about you poking round into Jackson's death? I expected you of all people to let my son rest, Reverend.'

Reverend Flowers stepped forward and spoke in a calm tone. 'Annabelle, I'm sorry if we've upset you. Yes, I went to visit my Chaplain who was with Jackson that day. Edward came with me for support.'

'That's not true, he went because *she* sent him. And you went to Jackson's school.'

The Chalk Gap grapevine never ceased to amaze me. 'How do you even know that?'

'It's all over the internet,' she snapped.

'Ah, did you see my posts about it?' Noah piped up. 'I hoped people would, I used hashtags and everything.'

I intercepted quickly before he started reeling off the hashtags he'd used. 'Annabelle, we're really sorry. We're not trying to cause any trouble. I've just been trying to help Mary get some closure.'

'Closure? What closure does it bring us trying to bring my other son into it?' she raged. 'Whatever you're doing, it needs to stop. Leave Jonathan to mourn his brother, and let Jackson rest in peace.' With that, she turned and stormed away.

We said our byes to Reverend Flowers, and I headed back to the pub with Noah to say hello to Mum.

'I wonder how she named her sons?' Noah mused as I half listened.

I once again had the nagging feeling something wasn't right but I couldn't put my finger on it. 'What are you talking about?'

'They're named differently. I've been learning about names in language on my A Level English course, I find it really interesting. Jonny is short for Jonathan but Jackson isn't short for anything. You'd think she'd have named them in a similar way. I wonder where she got the names from?'

I was barely listening but he continued, undeterred. 'Jackson might be named after Michael Jackson. Does she look like a Michael Jackson fan?'

I stopped now and gave him my full attention. 'Noah, what?'

'Sorry, we should focus on the case,' he said as he

smiled sheepishly. 'I just find ways of naming people really fascinating. I thought I was named after Noah's Ark but Mum said she just liked the name. I wonder why your mum chose the name Edward? Shall we ask her?... Edward, shall we ask her?'

Unfortunately for Noah (and I felt a little guilty afterwards), I'd tuned out again as he continued his endless monologue about names. My mind has drifted, processing everything we knew, and then I realised something: the key to this whole story. I knew what had happened to Jackson King, and who was responsible.

13

'Are you sure about this, mate?'

I'm not sure if I'd actually class DI Appleby as my 'mate' or not. As my old school bully, I didn't have the greatest past with him; as the Detective Inspector assigned to the two murder cases in Chalk Gap this past year, we had an interesting present. I think Appleby was moving towards grudging respect of the help I'd given him, and he was the first person I thought of to help me with the Jackson King case.

He'd driven straight over to Chalk Gap to hear my story, we'd come up with a plan and we were now arriving at Mary King's house.

'I said, are you sure about this, mate?' He repeated as I was lost in thought.

'Yes, yes,' I said as I took a nervous gulp. This was my third time now resolving a murder case and I could feel my anxiety rising. But I'd done this before and I knew I could do it again. 'You've definitely got back-up on the way?'

'Yes, mate, arriving in the village in a few minutes; they'll be ready on my signal.'

‘Let’s do this then.’ I knocked on the door to Mary’s cottage, which she opened straight away, no doubt waiting on tenterhooks for our arrival.

‘Edward, come in, come in,’ she muttered quickly as she ushered us in to her living room.

‘Mary, this is DI Appleby from Sussex Police,’ I said as we both took a seat on her sofa.

‘Hello, Officer. Thank you, both of you. What’s going on then? Do you have proof it’s him?’ Her words fired out of her mouth, almost too quickly to catch, as she paced backwards and forwards in front of us.

‘We’ll get to that in time,’ Appleby said, speaking for the first time. ‘Did you call him?’

‘Yes, he’s on his way. I said exactly what Edward told me to, he bought it. I don’t ever want to see that man again, but if it gets him locked away, I’ll do anything.’ She finally sat down on the other sofa opposite us.

We sat in awkward silence for a few moments, with the room quiet enough to hear a car engine outside. Mary jumped up and raced to the window. ‘He’s here.’ She addressed Appleby. ‘What should I do?’

‘Let him in. Don’t worry, I’ll be right here. Edward, go wait in the kitchen like we discussed.’

Mary firstly looked puzzled, and then nervous as she went to the door, but she wasn’t the only one. I’d taken a huge gamble: with both my theory itself, and involving DI Appleby and letting him do it his way. But this seemed like the best way to get the truth, once and for all.

Mary opened the door and I heard the voice on the other side of it before she even had chance to speak. 'What's this about, Mary? Weeks I've been trying to speak to you, and nothing. Then you send your spies sneaking around, and now this summons to come see you. I didn't have to come here, you know.'

'I knew you would though, Jonny,' I heard her reply. 'You can't resist.'

Neither can you,' he sniped. 'Can I come in now?'

I heard footsteps moving closer as Mary returned to the living room with Jonny.

'Wait, what's going on?' I heard him say, presumably at the sight of Appleby.

'Sussex Police, DI Appleby,' I heard, as I suppressed a grin, knowing he was flashing his police ID at that very moment. 'Just so you know who I am, before you even think about going for that door.'

'Mary, what the hell is the meaning of this?'

'Relax Jonny, you don't even know me.' I could tell Appleby was enjoying this. 'Let's rectify that, shall we? You've seen my ID, I wonder if you have any to show me?'

'No, not on me... what are you talking about?' I heard Jonny stutter. 'I just came to see my sister-in-law, like she asked. What's going on?'

'Ah, sorry, my fault that it's all a bit confusing,' Appleby said. 'I know how to clear it up. I should have said, I'm not here alone. I have a member of the public with me, a crucial witness.'

'What is this rubbish?' Jonny snapped. 'Witness to what?'

'Oh, I'd say wilful deception, at the very least. But see for yourself. I'd like you to meet a friend of mine.' There was a dramatic pause before he projected his voice towards where I hid in the kitchen. 'Come on in, Edward.'

'Wait, no, I can explain,' I heard Jonny mutter, much quieter and less sure now.

'What's to explain? The fact that you're already met Edward, haven't you, Jonny? Or should I say Jo*nathan*.'

I stepped into the room to see Nathan Foster.

14

'Mary, please can you confirm that this is the man you know as Jonny King?'

'What do you mean, the man I know as Jonny King? This *is* Jonny King. I've been unfortunate enough to know him for a long time.'

Appleby turned to me. 'And Edward, can you confirm that you met this man today as Nathan Foster, the chaplain volunteer who was with Jackson King in his last moments?' I nodded before Appleby stepped towards Nathan, or Jonny, or whatever I was supposed to call him.

'Nathan Foster, you are under arrest on suspicion of the murder of Jackson King. You do not have to say anything, but it may harm your defence if you do not mention when questioned something which you later rely on in court. Anything you do say may be given in evidence.'

Nathan simply shook his head to indicate that he wouldn't speak another word. It reminded me of Iago when he was caught out at the end of *Othello*.

Appleby started to lead him away, but my attention was on Mary, who screamed after him and lunged towards the door. 'Murderer! I knew it, I knew it!'

'It's okay, it's alright, they've got him now,' I reassured her as I put my hands on her shoulders to hold her back. She shrugged me off and collapsed onto the sofa in tears.

She cried for a few minutes as I awkwardly tried to comfort her. Eventually, she lifted her head and spoke to me. Why was the DI calling him Nathan? And how are you involved?'

I took a deep breath. 'Nathan is the volunteer Chaplain who was with Jackson in his final moments; I met him this morning. Him and Jonny are one and the same.'

She looked at me in disbelief. 'Sorry, what?'

'When Jonny left the village in disgrace all those years ago, he created a new identity for himself. Jo*nathan* King, as per his birth certificate with his mother's name, became Nathan Foster, using his father's surname.'

'How did you even work that out?' she asked, as she wiped her wet eyes with the side of her hand.

'My mum told me that their dad was always known as Fozzy, and that King was actually their mum's maiden name; she never married their father. If Fozzy is their father's nickname, it stands to reason that his surname was Foster.'

'Yes, I remember that,' she said as she sniffled.

I didn't make the connection when Reverend

Flowers showed me Nathan's ID, then I heard your mum refer to him as Jo*nathan*. But it was thanks to Noah's musings on naming methods that I pieced it together.'

'What are you talking about, ID?' Mary asked.

'For his plan to work, he had to be verified by Reverend Flowers to volunteer as a Chaplain. He had to prove he was who he said he was, and that he was of good character. The ID would have been easy; I imagine that he changed his name by deed poll to Foster years ago. Then, when I remembered that the Kings were a long time church-going family, I realised that the reference he provided from a Vicar in Eastbourne was also genuine. But they were practically the only things we learned about Nathan that were actually true.'

'What else did he tell you?' Mary asked, sounding quieter and more nervous.

'A lie that I couldn't put my finger on,' I replied. 'I knew something wasn't right about what he told me, but I couldn't work out exactly why at first. Then it hit me. His story was that he became a search and rescue Chaplain after his friend lost his life at our village cliffs last year. But I remembered afterwards why this didn't feel right; there hasn't been a death from our cliffs for about three years.'

Mary looked at me in shock. 'I can't believe he actually went to all these lengths. But, hang on a second, how did he fool Reverend Flowers? Didn't he recognise him?'

'Why would he?' I countered. 'Jonny left the village ten years ago, the Reverend told me that he'd never met him. He only knew *Nathan*, which had been proved by his driving licence. But he had to be careful when he attended the funeral as Jonny, which is why he sat at the back, wore sunglasses and made sure he'd started to grow a beard.'

'Let me guess, Nathan was clean shaven? This is insane. I can't believe he actually tried to get away with this stuff.' She threw herself back onto the sofa with her hands in the air in dramatic fashion. 'Go on then, what next?'

I smiled in sympathy and got ready to continue the story. 'Once he was established as a chaplain volunteer, had been through the training and started his patrols, he started to put his plan into place. On the day in question, before his shift, he left a handwritten note for Jackson at the school where he was working, presumably being careful not to be witnessed dropping it off. Then all he had to was wait.'

'Wait to murder his own brother,' Mary said in disgust.

I paused a moment, preparing myself to bring up the most difficult part of the conversation. 'I need to talk to you about what I think was in the note.'

'What do you mean?' she snapped. 'I just assume it was a note telling him to meet him on West Cliff.' I'd thought about this a lot and could only come to one conclusion. 'Why would Jackson leave work there and then, on receiving it? He would have probably ignored it. I think it also told him something else. Something that would make Jackson go straight up that cliff to confront his brother.'

'What do you think it was?' Mary asked, almost inaudible and with her eyes glued to the floor. I guessed that she knew what it was but was waiting for me to say it. 'Go on.'

'That Jackson isn't the father of your baby. Jonny is.'

15

I'd suspected Mary's affair with Jonny after the story about him seeing them buying the pregnancy test, and his renewed determination to make contact after that. Mary had already admitted to me that Jonny was the one who blabbed to Annabelle about the pregnancy, but that didn't explain how Jonny would have known that she was definitely pregnant. I'd also noted in her funeral dedication that she didn't mention him being a father.

The whole story just seemed to be more than the coincidence that Mary was playing it as, and would explain why Jonny had a renewed interest in the family in recent months, including trying to rekindle his relationship with his mother – who I suspected knew the baby secret and this was the reason for her new dislike of Mary.

Mary had finally broke down and admitted the affair to me, and that she wasn't sure which brother was the father. Mary's sister, Terri, returned with baby Joshua shortly after this, so I left her with her sister to look after her.

I was now in the pub with Reverend Flowers,

Mum and Noah, discussing the events of the case.

'I can't believe I fell for it, Edward. I feel such a fool. I'm so sorry.'

'You have nothing to be sorry for Reverend,' Mum said as she put the drinks down on the table. 'You had no way of knowing his true identity or true intentions.'

'Poor Mary was right all along, and none of us listened,' he continued. 'She *knew* Jonny had killed her husband.'

'It's a plot twist none of us could have known, though,' Noah added. 'It's really clever when you think about it.'

'I just don't know what kind of mind Jonny King had to plot to kill his own brother like that. And to think he could be the father of that baby.' Mum wasn't usually shocked by much, but this had even stunned her.

'I just hope they can get a conviction,' I said. 'Appleby said it might be difficult to prove that he actually murdered him, even though he plotted to get him up there. They might go for an Encouraging or Assisting Suicide charge instead. But even that carries up to 14 years.'

'Do you think he physically pushed him or incited him to jump? Mum asked.

I'd thought about this, and about Jonny's Iago style silence so far. It was possible that we would never know the truth.

‘Either way, he planned his brother’s death,’ Reverend Flowers asserted.

‘He needs locking up, the monster,’ Mum said. ‘Poor Mary, she’ll have to live with this forever now. And poor Annabelle, imagine one of your sons killing the other.’

‘I’ll pray for them,’ Reverend Flowers said. ‘And I have a few bereavement groups I can put them in touch with. Jackson suffered with mental health issues for a long time and I don’t want either of them to fall into that. I want them to process their grief and try to heal.’

‘I’m going to tell them that there’s no charge for the funeral buffet, it’s on the house,’ Mum added, which for her was a massive gesture. ‘And the pub are going to make a donation to your Chaplaincy search and rescue team, Reverend. Well, Casper is. He just doesn’t know it yet.’

This seemed the right time to make my suggestion to Reverend Flowers. ‘I guess that you’ll have a vacancy now on your search and rescue team. I’d like to apply for it, if I can.’

‘Edward, are you sure?’ Mum jumped in straight away. ‘I don’t like the thought of you wandering the cliffs like that.’

‘It’s a very challenging role, Edward,’ Reverend Flowers said. ‘But I expect you know that. And I think you’ll be fantastic at it.’

I’d known when I visited the graveyard yesterday

it was something I wanted to do. Helping investigating murders as an amateur was something I enjoyed doing, feeling that I had helped avenge someone's death. But I felt that if I was able to *prevent* death, and help people who desperately needed it, I should do it. I'd had my own problems with mental health and it seemed like the right thing to do.

'Then I think it's wonderful,' Mum said. 'I'm so proud of you, Edward.'

It felt like there was one thing left for us all to do. 'I just want to raise my glass to Jackson. May he rest in peace.'

I raised my glass and the others echoed my gesture, even Noah with his lemonade. 'To Jackson.'

THE EDWARD CRISP MYSTERIES – AVAILABLE ON AMAZON

AND COMING APRIL 2021...

PETER BOON
DEATH IN THE CLOSET
AN EDWARD CRISP MYSTERY

Printed in Great Britain
by Amazon

58624636R00047